THE
REAL ESTATE
PLAYBOOK

THE ESSENTIAL Q&A GUIDE
FOR BUYERS & SELLERS

ANGELA MIA DILORENZO

Published by Prominence Publishing, Inc.
www.prominencepublishing.com

The author can be reached as follows:
Phone: (231) 632-5105
Email: angelamiadilorenzo@bhhsmi.com
Website: www.michiganlifestylehomes.com

ISBN: 978-1-990830-45-7

"A home is one of the most important assets that most people will ever buy. Homes are also where memories are made, and you want to work with someone you can trust."

- Warren Buffet

DEDICATION

As I reflect on 25 remarkable years in the service of helping people navigate their real estate journeys, I am profoundly grateful for the many clients I have had the privilege of working with. Your trust, loyalty, and confidence — not to mention the invaluable referrals — have been the bedrock of my business. Your belief in my ability to guide you through one of life's most significant transitions has made this career deeply rewarding.

It is my pledge to continue providing the very best counsel, advice, and service, as I have always strived to do. You have not only been clients but partners in every success we have achieved together. For every smile, handshake, and set of keys exchanged, I am thankful. It is because of you that I love what I do, and it is to you that this book is dedicated.

Thank you for allowing me to be part of your story.

Angela Mia DiLorenzo

MY APPROACH TO REAL ESTATE

With 25 years of real estate expertise, I offer homeowners unparalleled guidance in selling their homes. My approach combines deep market insight, tailored marketing strategies, and a relentless commitment to achieving your selling goals. I pride myself on creating a smooth, transparent, and effective selling experience, ensuring your property successfully attracts top offers and closes. My commitment to you is rooted in a proven track record of successful sales and strategic marketing that ensures your property stands out. Choose a partner who not only lists your home but champions your interests, utilizes aggressive marketing techniques, and negotiates relentlessly on your behalf to secure the best possible outcome.

TABLE OF CONTENTS

INTRODUCTION

Hello and welcome! As a top real estate professional in Northern Michigan, I'm frequently asked countless questions by both buyers and sellers - from negotiating offers to staging advice to financing tips and more. After helping hundreds of clients successfully navigate the real estate process over my 20+ year career, I realized there was an opportunity to compile my expertise into an accessible guide for others.

That's why I wrote *The Real Estate Playbook*. Consider it your essential Q&A guide for tackling some of the most common questions facing buyers and sellers alike.

Inside, you'll discover straightforward answers surrounding topics like working with agents, avoiding mistakes, pricing homes, staging, inspections, contracts, and so much more. I cover both fundamental queries as well as some of the nuanced dilemmas my clients have brought to me over the years.

My goal is simple - to equip you with the knowledge and confidence you need to make the best decisions possible on your real estate journey. I believe that being an informed and empowered client is critical to achieving success whether you're buying or selling. There's a lot at stake, and having an expert coach on your side can make all the difference. I should know after personally helping hundreds of families buy and sell homes smoothly and for top dollar over my career.

Consider this book your personal playbook. A reference guide with helpful pointers as you navigate the real estate landscape. I'm always just a phone call or email away should you need any further assistance - it's what I love to do! But for now, dive in and soak up these home buying and selling insights I've curated just for you. Knowledge is power, my friend. I can't wait for it to help transform your real estate dreams into reality!

PART ONE: FOR BUYERS

WHAT ARE THE ADVANTAGES OF WORKING WITH A REAL ESTATE AGENT TO BUY A HOUSE?

There are several benefits to working with a real estate agent when buying a house:

✓ **Access to more properties:** Real estate agents have access to a wider range of properties on the market, including those that may not be publicly listed. They can also help you narrow down your search based on your specific requirements and preferences.

✓ **Expert knowledge**: A good real estate agent will have extensive knowledge of the local real estate market, including current prices, trends, and neighborhoods. This can help you make informed decisions about which properties to consider and how much to offer.

✓ **Negotiation skills:** Real estate agents are trained negotiators who can help you navigate the complex process of making an offer and closing a deal. They can advocate on your behalf to get you the best possible price and terms.

✓ **Paperwork and legal issues**: Buying a home involves a lot of paperwork and legal requirements, and a real estate agent can help you navigate these processes. They can ensure that all necessary documents are properly filled out and submitted, and can work with attorneys and other professionals as needed.

✓ **Professional network**: Real estate agents often have an extensive network of professionals who can assist with home inspections, repairs, and other services that may be needed during the buying process.

Overall, working with a real estate agent can help you save time, money, and stress when buying a home. They can guide you through the process, provide expert advice, and help ensure that your transaction goes smoothly.

WHAT ARE THE BIGGEST MYTHS OR MISCONCEPTIONS ABOUT THE HOME BUYING PROCESS?

There are several myths and misconceptions surrounding the home buying process, including:

× **You need a 20% down payment:** This is a common myth that many people believe. While having a 20% down payment can help you avoid private mortgage insurance (PMI), it's not always necessary. There are many mortgage programs available that allow for smaller down payments, including FHA loans, VA loans, and USDA loans.

× **Your credit has to be perfect:** While having good credit is important when buying a home, it doesn't have to be perfect. Many lenders will work with borrowers who have less-than-perfect credit scores. It's important to shop around and find a lender who will work with you.

× **You should buy the most expensive home you can afford:** It's easy to get caught up in the excitement of buying a new home and stretch your budget to buy the most expensive home you can afford. However, it's important to remember that buying a home is a long-term investment, and you don't want to be house poor. Make sure you're comfortable with your monthly mortgage payment and that you have room in your budget for unexpected expenses.

× **You don't need a home inspection:** Some home buyers may be tempted to skip the home inspection to save money or time. However, a home inspection is a crucial part of the home buying process. It can help identify any potential issues with the home that you may not have noticed during your initial walk-through.

× **You should always go with the lowest interest rate:** While getting a low interest rate on your mortgage is important, it's not the only factor to consider. You should also look at the overall cost of the loan, including any fees and closing costs. It's important to compare offers from multiple lenders to find the best deal for your situation.

WHAT ARE THE MOST COMMON MISTAKES HOMEBUYERS MAKE?

Some of the most common mistakes homebuyers make:

- × **Not getting pre-approved for a mortgage:** Before you start house hunting, it's important to get pre-approved for a mortgage so that you know how much you can afford to spend on a home. Not doing so can lead to disappointment when you find a house you love but can't afford.

- × **Not considering all the costs:** Many homebuyers focus only on the purchase price of the home and forget to factor in other costs like property taxes, homeowners' insurance, utilities, and maintenance costs. These expenses can add up quickly and may affect your ability to afford the home.

- × **Skipping the home inspection:** A home inspection is a crucial step in the homebuying process that can reveal any potential problems with the property. Skipping the inspection can lead to un-expected and expensive repairs down the road.

×   **Choosing the wrong location:** Location is key when it comes to buying a home. Make sure to research the neighborhood, schools, and ameni-ties before making a purchase. Choosing the wrong location can lead to dissatisfaction with your new home and even lower resale value.

×   **Letting emotions drive the decision:** Buying a home can be an emotional experience, but it's important to keep a level head and make a deci-sion based on your needs and financial situation. Don't let your emotions cloud your judgement and cause you to overspend on a home.

×   **Not having a realistic budget:** It's important to create a realistic budget before buying a home and sticking to it. This can help you avoid overspending and financial strain in the future.

×   **Not working with a reputable real estate agent:** A good real estate agent can help guide you through the homebuying process and offer valuable advice. Not working with an agent or choosing the wrong one can lead to a stressful and frustrating experience.

DO I REALLY NEED A REAL ESTATE AGENT TO BUY A HOME?

Working with a real estate agent when buying a home offers several advantages that can make the complex process much smoother and more efficient. Here are a few key benefits:

1. **Expert Guidance**: Real estate agents have a wealth of knowledge about the buying process, local market conditions, and negotiating tactics, which can be invaluable, especially for first-time buyers.

2. **Access to Listings**: Agents have access to comprehensive listings and can quickly find homes that match your criteria, saving you time and effort.

3. **Convenience and Time-Saving**: An agent can handle the legwork of scheduling showings, researching properties, and making inquiries on your behalf.

4. **Negotiation Skills**: Experienced agents can negotiate on your behalf to ensure you get the best possible price and terms. They know how to navigate bidding wars and can help you make competitive offers.

5. **Paperwork and Transactions**: There is a significant amount of paperwork involved in buying a home, and an agent can help ensure that everything is completed accurately and on time.

6. **Network of Professionals**: A real estate agent typically has a network of trusted professionals such as lenders, inspectors, and attorneys, which can be a great asset.

7. **Fiduciary Responsibility**: Your agent has a fiduciary duty to act in your best interests, offering peace of mind that they are committed to helping you make the best possible investment.

Remember, success in real estate relies on expertise and strong relational skills, which are at the heart of what a good real estate agent offers.

WHO PAYS THE REAL ESTATE AGENT FEES WHEN BUYING A HOME?

Typically, the seller pays the real estate agent fees when selling a home. These fees are usually a percentage of the final sale price and are negotiated between the seller and their listing agent before the home is put on the market. However, in some cases, the buyer may agree to pay a portion of the fees, such as in a dual agency arrangement where the same agent represents both the buyer and the seller.

It's important to discuss any fees or commissions with your agent or real estate lawyer before entering into a contract to buy or sell a home.

SHOULD I GET PRE-APPROVED FOR A LOAN BEFORE I START LOOKING FOR A HOUSE?

Yes, it is generally a good idea to get pre-approved for a loan before you start looking for a house. There are several benefits to getting pre-approved for a loan:

✓ **You will know your budget:** Getting pre-approved for a loan will give you a better under-standing of how much you can afford to spend on a house. This can help you focus your search on homes that are within your budget, saving you time and energy.

✓ **You will be taken more seriously by sellers:** When you are pre-approved for a loan, you are showing sellers that you are a serious buyer who has already taken steps to secure financing. This can give you an advantage in a competitive housing market.

✓ **You can move quickly:** If you find the perfect home, having pre-approval for a loan can help you move quickly to make an offer. This can be especially important in a fast-paced market where homes are selling quickly.

✓ **You can avoid disappointment:** If you start looking at homes without being pre-approved for a loan, you may fall in love with a home that is outside of your budget. Getting pre-approved for a loan can help you avoid the disappointment of finding your dream home only to realize you can't afford it.

Overall, getting pre-approved for a loan can be a smart move for anyone who is serious about buying a home. It can help you understand your budget, make a strong offer, and avoid disappointment.

ARE THERE SPECIAL PROGRAMS FOR FIRST-TIME HOME BUYERS?

Yes, there are special programs available for first-time homebuyers. These programs are designed to help first-time buyers get on the property ladder by offering assistance with down payments, closing costs, and other expenses associated with purchasing a home.

Some of the most common programs for first-time homebuyers include:

- ✓ **FHA Loans:** The Federal Housing Administration offers loans with lower down payments and easier credit requirements for first-time home-buyers.

- ✓ **VA Loans:** The Department of Veterans Affairs offers loans with zero down payment for eligible veterans, active-duty service members, and surviving spouses.

✓ **USDA Loans:** The U.S. Department of Agriculture offers loans for low-to-moderate-income borrowers in rural areas.

✓ **Good Neighbor Next Door:** This program offers eligible law enforcement officers, firefighters, emergency medical technicians, and teachers a 50% discount on the purchase price of a home in designated revitalization areas.

In addition to these federal programs, many states and local governments also offer first-time homebuyer programs that can help with down payment assistance, closing cost assistance, and other homebuying expenses. It's worth checking with your local government and housing authority to see what programs are available in your area.

HOW MUCH DOWN PAYMENT WILL I NEED?

A down payment is typically required to buy a house. The amount can vary depending on the type of loan you're securing and the lender's requirements.

Commonly, down payments range from 3.5% of the purchase price for an FHA loan, up to 20% or more for conventional loans if you want to avoid paying private mortgage insurance (PMI). Some specialized loan programs, such as VA loans for veterans or USDA loans for rural properties, may offer the possibility of zero down payment. It's important to consider that a larger down payment can reduce your monthly mortgage payment and potentially secure better loan terms.

When determining how much to save for a down payment, it's also essential to factor in additional costs like closing costs, moving expenses, and home maintenance. Considering these financial aspects carefully can help ensure that you're well-prepared for the home-buying process.

Not getting pre-approved has disadvantages:

Not getting pre-approved for a loan before shopping for a home can lead to several disadvantages in the buying process:

1. **Limited Budget Insight**: Without a pre-approval, you may not have a clear understanding of how much you can afford to spend on a home, which could lead to wasted time looking at homes outside of your budget.

2. **Less Attractive to Sellers**: Sellers often prefer buyers who have been pre-approved, as it provides evidence that they are serious and financially capable. Not having a pre-approval could make your offer less competitive, especially in a seller's market. As well as you may not be able to view some houses since the seller requires a pre-approval before allowing an in-person viewing.

3. **Potential for Heartbreak**: Falling in love with a home and then discovering you're unable to afford it can be emotionally challenging and can set back your home search significantly.

4. **Inefficiency in the Buying Process**: Being pre-approved speeds up the buying process because you've already provided your financial information to a lender, and they have assessed your creditworthiness.

5. **Risk of Longer Closing Times**: Without pre-approval, it might take longer to close on a house, as the loan approval process can be time-consuming. This delay could put you at risk of losing the home to another buyer who is ready to move forward quickly.

It' is a good idea to get pre-approved before you start house hunting. This helps ensure that you're looking at homes you can afford and can make a strong offer when you find the right property. If you need advice on how to improve your chances of getting pre-approved, that's something a skilled real estate coach can help with, equipping you with strategies and insights to enhance your financial readiness.

HOW DO I KNOW HOW MUCH I CAN AFFORD?

To determine how much you can afford, you will need to take a close look at your current financial situation. Here are some steps you can take:

1. **Evaluate your income:** Look at your monthly income after taxes. This will give you a better idea of how much money you have to work with.

2. **Determine your expenses:** List all your monthly expenses, including rent/mortgage, utilities, car payments, groceries, insurance, and any other regular bills. Subtract these expenses from your monthly income to get your disposable income.

3. **Calculate your debt-to-income ratio:** Your debt-to-income ratio is your monthly debt payments divided by your monthly income. Ideally, this ratio should be below 36%. If your ratio is higher, you

may want to consider paying off some debts before taking on new ones.

4. **Determine how much you can afford for housing:** As a general rule, your monthly housing costs should not exceed 28% of your gross monthly income. This includes mortgage/rent payments, property taxes, and insurance.

5. **Consider other expenses:** Remember to factor in other expenses, such as car payments, student loans, and credit card debt, when determining how much you can afford.

By following these steps, you can get a better under-standing of your financial situation and determine how much you can afford. It's important to be honest with yourself about your income, expenses, and debts so you don't end up overextending yourself financially.

WHAT ARE THE COSTS ASSOCIATED WITH BUYING A HOUSE?

Buying a house involves various costs that go beyond just the purchase price of the property. Here are some of the most common costs associated with buying a house:

- **Down payment:** This is the amount of money you pay upfront as a percentage of the purchase price. The down payment amount varies depending on the lender and the type of loan.

- **Closing costs:** These are the fees associated with processing the purchase of the property, including loan origination fees, title search fees, appraisal fees, and attorney fees.

- **Property taxes:** As a homeowner, you will be responsible for paying property taxes, which are typically based on the value of the property.

- **Homeowner's insurance:** Lenders typically require you to have homeowner's insurance, which protects your property and possessions from damage or theft.

- **Private mortgage insurance (PMI):** If your down payment is less than 20% of the purchase price, you may be required to pay PMI, which protects the lender in case you default on the loan.

- **Home inspection:** Before buying a house, it's important to have it inspected by a professional to identify any potential issues or needed repairs. The cost of a home inspection varies depending on the size of the property and location.

- **Appraisal fee:** The lender may require an appraisal of the property to ensure it's worth the purchase price. The cost of an appraisal varies depending on the property's value and location.

- **Moving expenses:** Once you've purchased the property, you'll need to pay for the costs associated with moving, such as hiring movers, renting a moving truck, and packing supplies.

It's important to factor in these costs when determining your budget for buying a house.

WHAT ARE THE MOST IMPORTANT THINGS TO LOOK FOR WHEN BUYING A HOME?

Buying a home is a major decision, and it's important to take the time to consider several factors before making a purchase. Here are some of the most important things to look for when buying a home:

- ✓ **Location:** The location of a home is one of the most important factors to consider. It can affect the home's value, safety, accessibility, and proximity to amenities such as schools, parks, shopping centers, and public transportation.

- ✓ **Price:** The price of a home is a crucial factor to consider when buying a home. It's important to have a clear idea of your budget and to stick to it. You should also consider the long-term costs associated with homeownership, such as property taxes, utilities, maintenance, and repairs.

✓ **Size and layout:** The size and layout of a home should meet your needs and lifestyle. Consider the number of bedrooms, bathrooms, and living spaces you need, as well as the overall layout and flow of the home.

✓ **Condition:** The condition of a home is another important factor to consider. A home inspection can help identify any major issues or repairs that may be needed before purchasing the home.

✓ **Resale value:** Even if you don't plan to sell your home in the near future, it's important to consider its resale value. Factors such as location, condition, and size can all impact the home's value and potential for resale.

✓ **Neighborhood:** The neighborhood in which a home is located can also impact its value and livability. Consider factors such as safety, accessibility, proximity to amenities, and the overall feel and character of the neighborhood.

Overall, buying a home requires careful consideration and research. By considering these important factors, you can make an informed decision and find a home that meets your needs and fits within your budget.

HOW MANY HOUSES SHOULD I LOOK AT BEFORE DECIDING TO PUT IN AN OFFER?

There is no set number of houses that you should look at before deciding to put in an offer. The number of houses you look at will depend on various factors such as your budget, the type of property you're looking for, the location you prefer, and the availability of homes on the market.

It's important to take the time to view multiple properties to get a sense of what's available and to compare the features, prices, and conditions of the homes you're interested in. This will help you make an informed decision when it comes to making an offer.

Ultimately, the number of houses you should look at will depend on your individual needs and preferences.

Take the time to do your research, visit open houses, and talk to real estate agents in your area to get a better sense of what's available and to help you make an informed decision.

Finding the right house is a blend of practical considerations and listening to your instincts. Here's how you can know if a house might be the right one for you:

1. **It Meets Your Essential Criteria**: You prepared a list of must-haves for your new home. If a house ticks all or most of the boxes on your list, it's a strong contender.

2. **You Can Afford It**: You feel comfortable with the price, and it aligns with your pre-approved loan amount without stretching your finances too thin.

3. **It Feels Like Home**: When you walk through the door, it feels welcoming. You can envision your life unfolding there, and it just 'feels right.'

4. **Good Location**: The location suits your needs in terms of commute, schools, amenities, and neighborhood culture.

5. **Good Condition**: The home is in good condition, or it's in a condition you're willing and able to manage, whether that means it's move-in ready or a fixer-upper that matches your abilities and budget for improvements.

6. **Future Potential**: It has potential for appreciation in value, or it meets long-term needs that will ensure it remains the right home for years to come.

7. **You're Already Planning the Move**: If you find yourself mentally arranging furniture or planning future renovations, it's a good sign that you're already invested in the house being your future home.

Remember, the "right" house will be different for everyone, depending on individual preferences, needs, and financial circumstances. Likewise, real estate coaching can help you refine your search strategy and decision-making skills to ensure you select a home that serves your best interests. Create a checklist for your home search, and make an appointment with both a lender and a professional real estate agent to help guide with your specific goals?

WHAT IS "EARNEST MONEY"?

An earnest money deposit is a sum of money that buyers put down as a show of good faith when entering into a real estate contract. It's essentially a way to demonstrate to the seller that the buyer is serious about purchasing the property. Here's how it typically works:

1. **Amount**: The amount of earnest money varies, but it's usually a percentage of the home's purchase price.

2. **Deposit**: The buyer deposits the earnest money into an escrow account after both parties agree to the terms of the sale and sign the contract. The funds are held by a third party, like a title company or real estate brokerage, until the transaction moves forward to closing.

3. **Protection for the Seller**: If the buyer backs out of the deal for reasons not covered by contingency clauses in the contract (like failing to sell a current home, get a mortgage, or unsatisfactory inspection), the seller may keep the earnest money as compensation for the time the property was off the market.

4. **Refund to Buyer**: If the transaction proceeds as planned, the earnest money is typically applied to the buyer's down payment or closing costs. If the contract has certain contingencies that aren't met, the earnest money is generally returned to the buyer.

5. **Contractual Role**: The terms regarding the earnest money deposit are outlined within the purchase agreement or contract, including the conditions under which it may be forfeited or refunded.

The earnest money deposit is part of the strategic considerations when making an offer and can play an influential role in competitive market conditions.

Understanding how to effectively use earnest money can be one of the many valuable insights you'll gain from a comprehensive coaching program in real estate. Would you like to know how you can strategically use earnest money in your offers to strengthen your position as a buyer?

How much should I put down?

The amount of earnest money you decide to put down can vary depending on several factors, including the local real estate market conditions, the demand for the property, and your level of interest in the home. Here are a few considerations to help you decide the appropriate amount:

1. **Standard Practice**: Learn about the typical amount for earnest money in your local market. This is often between 1% and 3% of the sale price but can be higher in very competitive markets.

2. **Signal Serious Intent**: A higher earnest money deposit may convey to the seller that you are more committed to the purchase, which can be particularly helpful in a competitive bid situation.

3. **Affordability**: Ensure the amount you're considering is within your financial means and that you're comfortable potentially risking it should the deal not proceed due to a contingency not being met.

4. **Seller's Expectation**: If the seller is expecting a standard amount and you offer more, this might give you an edge. Conversely, offering less may weaken your position.

5. **Negotiation Leverage**: The amount can sometimes be used as a negotiating tool. For example, you might offer a larger deposit to ask for certain concessions from the seller.

6. **Contingencies**: Ensure your offer includes appropriate contingencies to protect your earnest money should you need to back out of the sale for reasons such as a poor home inspection or inability to secure financing.

Deciding how much earnest money to offer is a strategic decision that can have implications for your home purchase. It can be beneficial to discuss this with a real estate coach who can provide guidance tailored to your specific situation and the current market conditions.

.

HOW LONG SHOULD I GIVE THE SELLER TO ACCEPT MY OFFER TO PURCHASE?

The amount of time you give a seller to respond to your offer can vary depending on a few factors, including market conditions, the urgency of the transaction, and customary practices in your area. Generally, it's common to give the seller 24 to 48 hours to respond to an offer.

However, in a very active market where properties move quickly, you might want to set a shorter deadline to expedite the process. Conversely, if the market is slower or if there are known complexities with the sale, you may choose to give the seller more time to consider.

It's important to communicate this timeframe clearly in your offer documents and be mindful of being reasonable and respectful of the seller's need to review the offer, especially if they are managing multiple interests or personal commitments.

Strategically determining the response time for your offer is one of the many nuanced skills that a real agent can help you refine. A real agent can give you insights into effective strategies for various market conditions to place you in the most advantageous position. Your Real estate agent will help you craft your offer in a way that balances assertiveness with flexibility.

WHAT HAPPENS IF MY OFFER IS REJECTED?

When an offer on a house is rejected, don't get dis-couraged; this is a common part of the real estate negotiation process. Here's what typically happens next:

1. **Review Feedback**: If the sellers provided any feedback on why the offer was rejected, carefully review it. This can give you valuable insight into what they are looking for and how you might be able to meet their needs with a revised offer.

2. **Evaluate Your Position**: If no feedback was provided, evaluate your offer's terms. Was it competitive? Did it meet the market conditions? You may also want to reassess your budget and how much you're willing to offer.

3. **Consider Your Options**:

- **Revise Your Offer**: Based on the feedback and your own evaluation, you may choose to submit a revised offer that's more appealing to the seller.

- **Move On**: Sometimes, it's not feasible to meet the seller's expectations due to financial constraints or differing values on the property's worth. In this case, it may be best to walk away and look for other opportunities.

4. **Consult a Professional**: A real estate professional or coach can provide advice on negotiation strategies and help you make an informed decision on whether to revise your offer or search for another property.

DO I NEED TO GET AN INSPECTION?

Yes, it is highly recommended that you get a home inspection when buying a house. A home inspection is a thorough examination of a property's condition by a professional inspector. The inspector will check the house's major systems and components, including the electrical, plumbing, heating and cooling, roof, foundation, and more, to identify any issues or potential problems.

Getting a home inspection can help you make an informed decision about whether to purchase the property and can also help you negotiate the price or request repairs before finalizing the sale. Additionally, a home inspection can give you a better understanding of the overall condition of the property and help you plan for any future maintenance or repairs.

IF THE INSPECTION REPORT COMES BACK WITH UNEXPECTED PROBLEMS, CAN I GET OUT OF THE CONTRACT?

It depends on the specific terms and conditions outlined in the contract. Generally, home purchase contracts include contingencies that allow the buyer to back out of the deal if certain conditions are not met. One common contingency is the inspection contingency, which allows the buyer to cancel the contract or negotiate repairs or credits based on the findings of the home inspection.

If the inspection report uncovers unexpected problems that are significant enough to cause the buyer to reconsider the purchase, they may be able to exercise their inspection contingency and either back out of the contract or renegotiate the terms. However, it's important to review the specific language of the contract and work with a real estate professional to understand the options and potential consequences before making a decision.

WHAT HAPPENS AFTER THE OFFER IS ACCEPTED?

Congratulations on having your offer accepted! Here's what generally happens after your offer on a house is accepted:

1. **Purchase Agreement:** You and the seller will sign a formal purchase agreement that outlines the terms of the sale, including price, contingencies, and the closing date.

2. **Escrow Begins:** The signed contract is sent to an escrow agent or attorney to begin the closing process. An earnest money deposit is typically required to secure the contract.

3. **Contingency Period:** If your offer included contingencies (such as financing, home inspection, appraisal, etc.), this is the time to fulfill them. You will need to get a home inspection, secure financing, and possibly have the home appraised.

4. **Secure Financing:** Work with your lender to finalize your mortgage, which includes submitting all necessary paperwork and going through the underwriting process.

5. **Title Search:** A title company will perform a search to ensure there are no issues with transferring ownership, such as liens or disputes.

6. **Final Walkthrough:** Before closing, you'll do a final walkthrough of the property to ensure that it's in the agreed-upon condition.

7. **Closing Day:** Assuming all contingencies are met and your financing is in place, you'll attend the closing meeting to sign all of the necessary paperwork, pay the remaining down payment and closing costs, and receive the keys to your new home.

HOW LONG DOES THE HOME BUYING PROCESS TAKE?

The home buying process can vary in duration depending on several factors, such as the specific circumstances of the buyer, the local housing market, and the type of financing used. However, on average, the home buying process takes between 30 to 60 days.

Here's a rough timeline of the home buying process:

1. **Pre-Approval:** The buyer gets pre-approved for a mortgage loan. This typically takes a few days to a week.

2. **House Hunting:** The buyer searches for a home that meets their needs and budget. The length of this stage varies, depending on the housing market and the buyer's criteria.

3. **Making an Offer:** Once the buyer finds a home they want to buy, they make an offer to the seller. Negotiations may take a few days to a week.

4. **Home Inspection:** The buyer schedules a home inspection to identify any issues with the property. The inspection typically takes a few hours to complete, and the buyer receives a report within a few days.

5. **Appraisal:** The lender orders an appraisal of the property to ensure that it's worth the amount of the loan. The appraisal typically takes a few days to a week.

6. **Closing:** Once all the conditions of the sale have been met, the buyer and seller sign the closing documents. This typically takes a few hours to complete, and the buyer receives the keys to the property at the end of the process.

Overall, the home buying process can take anywhere from 30 to 60 days, but it's important to keep in mind that there are many factors that can affect the timeline.

WHAT DOES A TITLE COMPANY DO?

A title company is a firm that provides title insurance and escrow services for real estate transactions. The primary role of a title company is to ensure that the title to a piece of property is clear and free of any liens, encumbrances, or defects that could affect the ownership or transfer of the property.

To accomplish this, a title company conducts a thorough search of public records to identify any outstanding claims or issues related to the property. Once the title is deemed clear, the company issues a title insurance policy to protect the new owner from any potential future claims on the property.

In addition to title insurance, many title companies also offer escrow services, which involve holding funds in trust until all aspects of a real estate transaction have been completed, including the transfer of the property and payment of all fees and expenses. The title company typically acts as a neutral third party in these transactions, ensuring that all parties involved receive what they are owed and that the transaction is completed smoothly and efficiently.

WHAT ARE THE BIGGEST MISTAKES HOMEBUYERS MAKE?

Here are some of the biggest mistakes homebuyers make:

- × **Failing to get pre-approved for a mortgage:** Before beginning your home search, it's important to get pre-approved for a mortgage so you know what you can afford. This will also help you avoid falling in love with a home that's outside of your budget.

- × **Skipping the home inspection:** A home inspection can reveal potential issues with the home that could end up costing you a lot of money down the line. Skipping this step can be a costly mistake.

- × **Not shopping around for the best mortgage rate:** Many homebuyers don't realize that they can shop around for the best mortgage rate. This can end up costing you thousands of dollars over the life of your loan.

× **Making emotional decisions:** Buying a home can be an emotional process, but it's important to keep your emotions in check and make decisions based on logic and reason. Don't let your emotions lead you to make a hasty decision.

× **Ignoring additional costs:** There are many additional costs associated with buying a home, including closing costs, property taxes, and home insurance. It's important to factor these costs into your budget so you're not caught off guard.

× **Failing to consider the neighborhood:** The neighborhood you buy in can have a big impact on your quality of life. Make sure to research the neighborhood and take into account factors like schools, commute times, and local amenities.

× **Overlooking potential resale value:** While you may not be thinking about selling your home when you buy it, it's important to consider its potential resale value. This can help ensure that you're making a good investment that will appreciate over time.

WHAT IS A HOME WARRANTY?

A home warranty is a service contract that provides coverage for the repair or replacement of certain appliances and systems in a home. Typically, a homeowner purchases a home warranty from a provider and pays an annual premium in exchange for coverage of specified items, such as heating and cooling systems, plumbing and electrical systems, and major appliances like refrigerators and ovens.

If an item covered by the warranty breaks down or malfunctions, the homeowner can submit a claim to the warranty provider, who will arrange for a qualified technician to make the necessary repairs or replace the item, depending on the terms of the warranty. Home warranties can provide peace of mind to homeowners, particularly those with older homes or appliances that may be more prone to breakdowns.

WHAT ARE SOME THINGS I SHOULD KNOW ABOUT A HOUSE BEFORE I MAKE AN OFFER?

Before making an offer on a house, there are several things you should know to ensure that you're making an informed decision. Here are some important factors to consider:

✓ **Condition of the house**: You should inspect the property to determine its overall condition. Look for any structural issues, signs of water damage or mold, electrical or plumbing problems, and the age and condition of major appliances and systems such as the HVAC, water heater, and roof.

✓ **Location:** Consider the location of the house in relation to your work, schools, shopping, and other amenities. Also, research the neighborhood to see if it's a good fit for your lifestyle and whether the area is safe and desirable.

✓ **Price:** Research the local real estate market to determine the fair market value of the property. Consider factors such as the age and condition of the property, the size of the lot, and the local real estate market conditions.

✓ **History of the property:** Look into the history of the property, including any previous owners, renovations or repairs made, and any issues with the property's title or ownership.

✓ **Taxes and fees:** Research the property taxes and any other fees associated with owning the property, such as homeowner's association fees, to ensure that they fit within your budget.

✓ **Financing options:** Determine your financing options, including your credit score, down payment, and interest rates, to determine the feasibility of purchasing the property.

✓ **Market conditions:** Consider the current real estate market conditions, including inventory levels, interest rates, and economic factors, to determine whether it's a good time to make an offer.

HOW DOES A REAL ESTATE AGENT HELP ME DURING THE HOME BUYING PROCESS?

A real estate agent can be a valuable asset during the home buying process in several ways:

- ✓ **Finding suitable properties:** A real estate agent can help you find properties that match your requirements, budget, and preferences. They can also help you narrow down your search by providing insights into the local real estate market and available properties.

- ✓ **Negotiating the price:** A real estate agent can help you negotiate the price of the property with the seller or their agent. They can use their knowledge of the local market and their negotiation skills to help you get the best deal.

- ✓ **Handling paperwork:** The home buying process involves a lot of paperwork, including contracts, disclosures, and other legal documents. A real estate agent can help you navigate through the paperwork and ensure that everything is in order.

✓ **Coordinating with other professionals:** A real estate agent can also coordinate with other professionals involved in the home buying process, such as home inspectors, appraisers, and mortgage lenders, to ensure that everything runs smoothly.

✓ **Providing guidance and advice:** Buying a home can be a complicated process, and it's normal to have questions and concerns along the way. A real estate agent can provide you with guidance and advice based on their experience and know-ledge of the real estate market, helping you make informed decisions throughout the process.

Overall, a real estate agent can make the home buying process smoother, faster, and less stressful, and can help you find the right home at the right price.

WHAT ARE SOME OF YOUR TOP TIPS WHEN LOOKING AT A HOUSE?

Here's what to look for:

✓ **Location:** The location of a house is crucial. Consider proximity to your work, schools, transportation, shops, and services. Also, consider the neighborhood and the safety of the area.

✓ **Size and Layout:** Determine whether the size and layout of the house will meet your needs. Consider the number of bedrooms, bathrooms, and the general layout of the living space.

✓ **Condition:** Check the condition of the house, including the roof, walls, and foundation. Check for signs of water damage, mold, or pests. Look for any repairs that need to be done, which can help you avoid unexpected expenses.

✓ **Natural light and ventilation:** A house with plenty of natural light and good ventilation is more desirable. Open windows and doors to check the flow of air.

✓ **Storage space:** Ensure the house has enough storage space for your belongings. Look for closets, cabinets, and storage spaces.

✓ **Outdoor space:** If outdoor space is essential to you, consider the size of the yard or garden, the land-scaping, and any outdoor features like a pool, patio, or deck.

✓ **Energy efficiency:** Look for energy-efficient features like double-pane windows, insulation, and energy-efficient appliances. They can save you money on your energy bills and help the environment.

✓ **Home inspection:** Consider hiring a professional home inspector to check the property for any hidden issues. An inspection can uncover potential prob-lems that could cost you later.

Remember, buying a house is a significant investment, and it's essential to take your time and thoroughly evaluate each property before making a decision.

The Value of a Buyer's Agent

The value that a great buyer's agent brings to the home-buying journey is unparalleled. A well-trained and dedicated buyer's agent is an advocate, educator, and confidant throughout the intricate process of purchasing a home. They tailor their expert services to satisfy the nuanced needs of homebuyers, offering a combination of support and expertise crucial for a smooth transaction. Here's a refined expression of their contribution:

Expertise and Advocacy: A great buyer's agent is not just a guide but a staunch advocate for your unique requirements. They engage in in-depth conversations, offering tailored advice and resources. Their rich insights into market conditions help you discern property values and make strategic decisions, ensuring you feel supported and protected throughout the process.

Efficient Property Discovery: Your time is precious, and a competent agent understands this. They meticulously source properties that align with your wishes, going beyond simply opening doors. With their extensive network, they can provide access to properties that are sometimes not yet on the market, giving you a competitive edge and making you feel that your time is respected and valued.

Negotiating and Strategizing: A professional buyer's agent comes equipped with sharp negotiating skills and a profound understanding of contracts. This enables them to negotiate favorable terms and navigate complex legal terms, ensuring your interests are legally protected.

Handling Logistics: Real estate transactions can be overwhelming, with multiple deadlines and extensive paperwork. Your agent takes on the responsibility of managing these critical timelines, from offer submissions to contingency removals, ensuring no detail is overlooked. This allows you to focus on other aspects of the process, relieving you of unnecessary stress and burden.

Continuous Support: Communication is vital in any transaction. A dedicated buyer's agent establishes continuous dialogue, keeping you informed at each stage of the buying process and providing support for any queries or concerns that might arise.

Post-Closing Assistance: Even after closing, a full-time, professional agent remains a valuable resource. They assist with post-purchase questions and can offer recommendations for any future real estate needs.

The following list further exemplifies specific actions a buyer's agent undertakes to secure your dream home:

- Organizes a strategy session to customize your home search plan.

- Prepares and presents educational material regarding the buying process.

- Advises on agency relationships and represents your best interests.

- Discusses various financing options and assists in finding suitable mortgage lenders.

- Provides resources to investigate neighborhood safety, school performance, and other pivotal factors.

- Regularly updates you on changing market conditions, new listings, and price adjustments.

- Offers clear, expert explanations on earnest money, contingencies, and the home inspection process.

- Expertly handles the many moving parts of a sales contract negotiation and execution.

By selecting an agent committed to their profession, you gain more than a mediator; you receive a full-time loyal partner dedicated to finding you not just a house but a home. They differentiate themselves through an unwavering commitment to your satisfaction, adapting to your unique needs with experience, empathy, and a thorough understanding of the real estate market.

PART TWO: FOR SELLERS

WHAT ARE THE BENEFITS OF WORKING WITH A REAL ESTATE AGENT TO SELL MY HOUSE?

The number one reason to use a realtor when selling a house is expertise and access to a wide range of professional resources. Realtors provide in-depth market knowledge, proven marketing strategies, negotiation skills, and expertise in handling the transaction's legal and procedural aspects.

A realtor can help accurately price your home, prepare it for sale, and list it to maximize exposure. They can effectively screen potential buyers, handle the complexities of offers and counteroffers, and navigate the closing process, ensuring everything is in order and in compliance with legal requirements. In essence, a realtor can be instrumental in securing the best possible outcome for the sale of your home, minimizing stress and potential setbacks for the seller.

WHAT ARE THE BIGGEST MYTHS OR MISCONCEPTIONS ABOUT SELLING A HOUSE?

There are several myths and misconceptions surrounding the home selling process. Here are some of the most common ones:

Myth: You need to make major renovations to sell your home.

Many people believe that they need to invest in expensive renovations to sell their home, but this is not always the case. While some updates can help increase your home's value, there are plenty of affordable ways to improve your home's appeal to buyers, such as decluttering, deep cleaning, and staging.

Myth: You should price your home high to leave room for negotiation.

Some sellers believe that setting a high asking price will give them more room to negotiate, but this can actually deter potential buyers. Overpriced homes often sit on the market for longer, and buyers may assume that there is something wrong with the property.

Myth: You don't need to disclose problems with the home.

Many sellers believe that they can hide defects or problems with their home from potential buyers, but this is not legal or ethical. Sellers are required to disclose any known issues with the property, such as leaks, pests, or structural problems.

Myth: You should only work with a real estate agent who suggests the highest listing price.

Some sellers choose to work with real estate agents who suggest a high listing price, thinking that this will result in a higher sale price. However, an experienced agent will know the local market and be able to provide a more accurate estimate of your home's value.

Myth: You should wait until spring or summer to list your home.

While spring and summer are popular times to sell a home, there is no one-size-fits-all answer to the best time to list. In some markets, it may be advantageous to list during a slower season when there is less competition.

Overall, it's important to do your research and work with professionals who can help guide you through the home selling process.

WHAT ARE THE MOST COMMON MISTAKES HOMEOWNERS MAKE WHEN SELLING THEIR HOUSE?

- **Overpricing the property:** One of the most common mistakes homeowners make is overpricing their home. Overpricing can scare away potential buyers and result in the property sitting on the market for an extended period, which can ultimately result in a lower sale price.

- **Neglecting necessary repairs and maintenance:** Failing to address necessary repairs and maintenance can hurt a home's sale price. Buyers may see the property as a fixer-upper and, therefore, expect a lower price or move on to another home.

- × **Failing to stage the home:** Home staging is the process of making a property more visually appealing to potential buyers. Failing to stage a home can make it difficult for buyers to envision themselves living in the space and can result in lower offers.

- × **Ignoring curb appeal:** First impressions matter, and the exterior of a home is the first thing potential buyers see. Neglecting curb appeal, such as overgrown landscaping, chipped paint, or cluttered yards, can turn buyers off before they even step inside.

- × **Refusing to negotiate:** While it's understandable to want to get the best price for your home, refusing to negotiate can limit your potential buyer pool and extend the time your property is on the market.

- × **Not hiring a real estate agent:** While it's possible to sell your home without a real estate agent, hiring a professional can help you navigate the complex process of selling a home and help you avoid costly mistakes.

- × **Not being flexible with showings:** Homeowners who refuse to be flexible with showing times can limit the number of potential buyers who see the property. Being accommodating with showing requests can increase the chances of selling your home quickly and at a desirable price.

× **Failing to disclose important information:** Sellers are required to disclose any known issues with the property, such as water damage, pest problems, or foundation issues. Failing to disclose such information can lead to legal trouble down the road and harm your reputation as a seller.

DO I REALLY NEED A REAL ESTATE AGENT TO SELL MY HOUSE?

No, you do not necessarily need a real estate agent to sell your home. However, there are several benefits to working with a professional real estate agent.

Firstly, real estate agents have a wealth of experience and expertise in the field, which can be invaluable when it comes to pricing, marketing, and negotiating the sale of your home. They can provide you with valuable insights into the local housing market and help you determine the best price for your property.

Secondly, real estate agents can help you market your home effectively, using a variety of channels to reach potential buyers. They can create professional listings, host open houses, and showcase your home on popular real estate websites.

Thirdly, real estate agents can handle all of the paper-work and legalities involved in selling a home, saving you time and hassle. They can help you navigate complex contracts, disclosures, and other legal documents to ensure a smooth and successful transaction.

Ultimately, whether you choose to work with a real estate agent to sell your home depends on your personal preferences and circumstances. If you are comfortable taking on the responsibilities of selling your home yourself, and have the time and expertise to do so, then you may be able to save on commission fees by selling your home without an agent. However, if you value the guidance, expertise, and peace of mind that comes with working with a professional real estate agent, then it may be worth the investment to hire one.

WHAT ARE THE ADVANTAGES OF BUYING A HOME VERSUS RENTING?

Buying a home has several advantages over renting, including:

- ✓ **Equity:** When you buy a home, you build equity in the property as you pay off the mortgage. This equity can be used in the future to take out a loan or sell the property for a profit.

- ✓ **Stability**: When you own a home, you have more stability and control over your living situation. You can make changes to the property, and you don't have to worry about a landlord raising the rent or asking you to move out.

- ✓ **Tax benefits:** Homeownership comes with tax benefits, including deductions for mortgage interest, property taxes, and other expenses related to owning a home.

✓ **Potential for appreciation**: Home prices can appreciate over time, meaning the value of your property could increase, potentially providing you with a significant return on investment.

✓ **Personalization**: When you own a home, you have the freedom to make changes to the property to fit your personal style and needs.

However, there are also some disadvantages to buying a home, including the upfront cost of a down payment, closing costs, and ongoing maintenance and repair expenses. It's important to consider both the advantages and disadvantages of homeownership before making a decision.

WHAT ARE THE COSTS ASSOCIATED WITH SELLING A HOUSE?

The costs associated with selling a house can vary depending on several factors such as location, market conditions, and the services you choose to use. Here are some common costs associated with selling a house:

- **Real estate agent commission:** If you choose to work with a real estate agent, they will typically charge a commission based on the sale price of the house, which can range from 2.5% to 6% of the sale price.

- **Home repairs and renovations**: You may need to make repairs or upgrades to your home before putting it on the market. These costs can vary widely depending on the age and condition of your home.

- **Staging and photography**: Many sellers choose to have their home staged and professionally photographed to make it more appealing to potential buyers. These services can cost several hundred to several thousand dollars.

- **Closing costs:** When the sale is complete, you may be responsible for paying closing costs, which can include fees for things like the title search, transfer taxes, and attorney fees.

- **Pre-sale inspections:** You may choose to have a home inspection, pest inspection, or other inspections done before putting your home on the market. These inspections can help identify any issues that need to be addressed before listing the property.

- **Property taxes and utilities:** You'll need to continue paying property taxes and utilities until the sale is complete, which can add up to a significant cost over time.

It's important to factor in these costs when calculating how much you can expect to make from the sale of your home.

SHOULD I SELL MY CURRENT HOME BEFORE BUYING A NEW HOUSE?

Whether or not you should sell your current home before buying a new one depends on several factors, including your financial situation, your goals, and the current state of the real estate market.

One advantage of selling your current home before buying a new one is that you will know exactly how much money you have available to put towards your new home purchase. This can help you avoid financial stress and uncertainty when it comes to making an offer on a new home.

On the other hand, if you sell your current home before finding a new one, you may need to find temporary housing or be in a rush to find a new home, which can lead to making hasty decisions or overpaying for a property.

If you are in a seller's market where homes are selling quickly and for high prices, it may make more sense to sell your current home first to take advantage of the favorable market conditions. However, if you are in a buyer's market where there are more homes available than buyers, it may be easier to find a new home first and then sell your current home.

Ultimately, the decision to sell your current home before buying a new one should be based on your personal circumstances and goals. It may be helpful to speak with a financial advisor or a real estate agent to help you weigh your options and make the best decision for your situation.

WHEN IS THE BEST TIME TO SELL MY HOUSE?

Determining the best time to sell a house can depend on various factors such as the local real estate market conditions, the condition of your home, your personal financial goals, and your personal circumstances. However, here are some general considerations to keep in mind:

- **Seasonality:** Typically, spring and summer are the peak seasons for home sales. However, this may vary depending on the local market conditions. In some areas, winter may be a good time to sell as there may be less competition.

- **Market Conditions:** Keep an eye on the local real estate market and assess the demand for homes in your area. If the market is hot, with high demand and low inventory, it could be a good time to sell.

- **Personal Circumstances:** Consider your personal circumstances such as job changes, family needs, or financial goals, and how they may affect your decision to sell.

- **Condition of your home:** Ensure that your home is in good condition before putting it on the market. This may involve minor repairs, upgrades, or a fresh coat of paint.

Ultimately, it's best to consult with a local real estate agent who can give you personalized advice based on your specific situation and market conditions in your area.

WHAT STEPS SHOULD I TAKE TO PREPARE MY HOME FOR SALE?

Preparing a house for sale can be a time-consuming and stressful process, but it can also help you to achieve the best possible sale price. Here are some steps you can take to prepare your house for sale:

- **Declutter:** Remove any unnecessary items and personal belongings from your home. Consider donating or selling items that you no longer need.

- **Deep clean**: Make sure your home is clean and tidy from top to bottom, including windows, floors, carpets, and walls. Consider hiring a professional cleaner to help with this task.

- **Repairs and maintenance**: Fix any minor issues around your home, such as leaking faucets, cracked tiles, or peeling paint. Also, make sure that all appliances and systems are in working order.

- **Depersonalize**: Remove any personal items, such as family photos or memorabilia. This can help potential buyers to imagine themselves living in your home.

- **Neutralize**: Consider painting your home with neutral colors, such as white or beige. This can help to create a clean and fresh look that appeals to a wide range of buyers.

- **Staging**: Consider hiring a professional stager to help showcase your home's best features and create an inviting atmosphere.

- **Curb appeal**: Make sure the exterior of your home is attractive and well-maintained. Consider adding some plants or flowers to create a welcoming entrance.

By following these steps, you can help your home to stand out from the competition and attract potential buyers.

WHAT CAN I DO IF I NEED TO SELL MY HOUSE FAST?

If you need to sell your house fast, there are several steps you can take to expedite the process:

- **Price your home correctly:** Setting the right price is critical to selling your house quickly. Research the local real estate market to ensure that you are pricing your home competitively.

- **Make necessary repairs and improvements:** Consider making repairs or improvements to your home that will make it more attractive to potential buyers. This may include painting, replacing outdated fixtures, or upgrading appliances.

- **Stage your home:** Staging your home can help potential buyers visualize themselves living in the space. Remove clutter, depersonalize the space, and add some tasteful decorations.

- **Hire a reputable real estate agent:** A good real estate agent can help you navigate the selling process and find potential buyers quickly.

- **Market your home effectively:** Use a variety of marketing strategies to get the word out about your home. This may include online listings, open houses, and targeted advertising.

- **Consider selling to a cash buyer:** If you need to sell your home quickly and don't want to go through the traditional selling process, consider selling to a cash buyer. These companies will purchase your home as-is, without the need for repairs or staging.

Remember that selling your home quickly may require you to be flexible with your asking price or terms of sale. Be prepared to negotiate with potential buyers to find a solution that works for both parties.

WHAT SHOULD I DO TO PREPARE MY HOUSE FOR SHOWINGS?

If you're preparing your house for showings, there are several things you can do to make your property more attractive to potential buyers. Here are some tips:

- **Clean and declutter:** A clean and tidy home is essential when you're trying to sell. Remove any unnecessary items and tidy up your belongings to make your house look more spacious and inviting.

- **Depersonalize:** Remove any personal items like family photos, religious or political items, and other personal effects to help potential buyers envision themselves living in the space.

- **Enhance curb appeal:** The first impression of your home is the exterior, so make sure it looks its best. Keep the lawn mowed and trim shrubs, add some fresh flowers or plants, and touch up any paint or repairs that are needed.

- **Repair any damages:** Fix any damages or defects that may be present in the house. This includes things like leaky faucets, broken windows, or damaged flooring.

- **Brighten up the space:** Let in natural light by opening curtains and blinds, add lighting fixtures or lamps to brighten up darker spaces, and consider painting walls in lighter, neutral colors to make rooms feel more open.

- **Make your home smell pleasant:** Use air fresheners, candles, or diffusers to make your home smell fresh and clean. Avoid using over-powering scents or anything that could be offensive to potential buyers.

By following these tips, you can make your home more attractive to potential buyers and increase the chances of a successful showing.

SHOULD I BE PRESENT DURING SHOWINGS AT MY HOME?

The answer depends on your personal preferences and the policies of your real estate agent.

In most cases, it is not necessary for you to be present during a property showing if you have a real estate agent. Your agent can coordinate with the buyer's agent to schedule and conduct the showing. This can save you time and make the process more convenient, especially if you have a busy schedule.

However, if you prefer to be present during the showing, you can certainly request to do so. Some sellers feel more comfortable being on hand to answer questions and provide information about the property. Be mindful the potential buyer may not feel comfortable If you are there.

Ultimately, it is up to you and your real estate agent to decide whether you should be present during property showings. Your agent can provide guidance on best practices and help you decide based on your individual circumstances.

HOW DO I KNOW HOW MUCH MY HOME IS WORTH?

There are several ways to estimate the value of your house, including:

- **Online Valuation Tools**: You can use online real estate valuation tools such as Zillow, Redfin, or Trulia to get an estimate of your home's value. These tools use public data, such as recent home sales and property tax assessments, to estimate your home's worth. Often these valuation tools are not accurate.

- **Comparative Market Analysis (CMA):** You can request a CMA from a real estate agent or broker in your area. A CMA will analyze recent sales of similar homes in your area to determine an estimated value for your home.

- **Professional Appraisal**: You can hire a licensed appraiser to conduct a professional appraisal of your home. Appraisers typically charge several hundred dollars for their services, but they will provide a detailed report that includes an estimated value for your home.

- **Consideration of Improvements**: You should also consider any recent improvements you've made to your home, such as a new roof or renovated kitchen, as these upgrades can increase your home's value.

Ultimately, the value of your home will depend on several factors, including its location, size, age, and condition. It's a good idea to use multiple methods to estimate your home's value to get a more accurate estimate.

CAN'T I FIGURE OUT HOW MUCH MY HOME IS WORTH FROM REAL ESTATE WEBSITES?

I do not suggest using them if you are looking for true value.

Online valuation tools are not always accurate because they use algorithms and public data to estimate the value of your home. While they can provide a general idea of what your home might be worth, they are not as accurate as a professional appraisal, or a comparative market analysis conducted by a real estate agent.

Online valuation tools may not take into account factors such as the condition of your home, any upgrades or renovations you've made, or unique features that may affect its value. They also cannot take into account local market trends or conditions, which can have a signifi-cant impact on the value of your home.

Additionally, online valuation tools may not have access to the most up-to-date information about your property, and their estimates may not be as reliable in areas where the real estate market is less active or where there are few comparable properties available.

Overall, online valuation tools can provide a helpful starting point for estimating the value of your home, but they should not be relied upon as the sole source of information. It's always a good idea to consult with a real estate professional or a licensed appraiser for a more accurate and reliable estimate of your home's value.

HOW DO I DECIDE ON WHAT PRICE TO LIST MY HOME FOR?

Deciding on the right price to list your house for can be a complex process that requires careful consideration of several factors. Here are some steps you can take to help you determine the right price for your home:

- **Conduct a market analysis**: Start by researching the local housing market and analyzing the prices of similar homes in your area. Look at recently sold properties in your neighborhood, as well as homes currently on the market that are similar to yours in terms of size, age, and features.

- **Consider the condition of your home**: The condition of your home can have a significant impact on its value. Be honest with yourself about any repairs or upgrades that may be needed and factor those into your pricing decision.

- **Evaluate your location**: The location of your home can also influence its value. Take into account factors like proximity to schools, shopping, transportation, and other amenities that may be important to potential buyers.

- **Determine your timeline**: How quickly do you need to sell your home? If you need to sell quickly, you may need to price your home competitively to attract buyers. However, if you have more time, you may be able to afford to wait for a higher offer.

- **Consult with a real estate agent**: A real estate agent can provide valuable insight into the local housing market and help you determine the right price for your home. They can also help you navigate the process of preparing your home for sale and marketing it to potential buyers.

Overall, determining the right price for your home requires careful consideration of several factors. By doing your research, being honest about the condition of your home, and seeking the advice of a professional, you can make an informed decision that will help you sell your home quickly and at the right price.

WHAT IS A CMA?

In the context of real estate, CMA stands for "Comparative Market Analysis." It is a report prepared by a real estate agent or broker to help determine the appropriate listing price for a property.

The CMA compares the subject property to similar properties that have recently sold, are currently on the market, or were listed but did not sell. The goal is to determine a fair market value for the property based on the current market conditions and the characteristics of the property being analyzed.

The CMA typically includes a detailed analysis of the property's features, such as the number of bedrooms and bathrooms, square footage, and amenities. It may also take into account the property's location, the local real estate market, and recent sales of comparable properties in the area.

The CMA is an essential tool for sellers looking to price their property competitively and attract potential buyers, and for buyers looking to make an informed offer based on current market conditions.

DO I NEED TO PROVIDE BUYERS' PERMITS OR OTHER DOCUMENTATION FOR IMPROVEMENTS I'VE MADE TO MY HOME?

It depends on the type of improvements you have made to your home and the regulations in your area.

If you have made significant changes to your home, such as adding rooms or making structural changes, you may need to obtain building permits from your local government. These permits ensure that your home improvements meet safety and zoning requirements. When you sell your home, potential buyers may ask for documentation to show that the improvements were made in compliance with local building codes and regulations.

Additionally, if you have made upgrades or improvements to your home that could affect its value, such as installing new electrical wiring, plumbing, or HVAC systems, you may want to keep records of the work done and any permits obtained. This can help potential buyers understand the value of the upgrades and the quality of the workmanship.

In summary, it is a good idea to keep documentation of any significant improvements made to your home, particularly those that required permits, as potential buyers may request this information during the sale process.

WHAT AM I REQUIRED TO DISCLOSE ABOUT MY HOUSE TO POTENTIAL BUYERS?

As a seller, you are typically required to disclose any known material defects or issues with the property to potential buyers. Material defects are those that would affect the property's value or pose a safety risk to occupants.

Some common examples of material defects include:

- Structural issues such as foundation problems or roof leaks

- Issues with plumbing, electrical or HVAC systems

- Water damage or mold problems

- Pest infestations

- Environmental hazards such as lead paint or asbestos

In addition to these material defects, you may also be required to disclose any known zoning violations, property line disputes, or other legal issues related to the property.

It's important to note that disclosure requirements vary by state and even by locality, so it's best to consult with a real estate attorney or agent in your area to ensure you are meeting all legal obligations.

WHAT IF HAVE LIENS OR OWE BACK TAXES ON MY HOUSE?

If you have liens or owe back taxes on your house, it is important to address these issues as soon as possible. Liens and back taxes can lead to serious consequences, including foreclosure and legal action. Here are some steps you can take:

- **Find out exactly how much you owe:** Contact your local government or tax authority to find out the exact amount you owe in back taxes or liens.

- **Work out a payment plan:** In many cases, you may be able to work out a payment plan with the government or the lien holder to pay off the debt over time.

- **Prioritize the debts:** If you have multiple debts on your property, prioritize the most urgent ones. For example, if you are facing foreclosure, focus on paying off that debt first.

- **Consider getting professional help**: If you are struggling to manage your debts, consider getting professional help from a financial advisor, a tax attorney, or a real estate professional.

- **Sell your property**: As a last resort, you may need to consider selling your property to pay off your debts. Selling your property may also help you avoid foreclosure and other legal actions.

In any case, it is important to take action quickly to address your liens or back taxes. Ignoring these issues can only make them worse and may lead to serious consequences in the long run.

IS THE TAX ASSESSED VALUE OF MY HOUSE ACCURATE?

In general, tax assessed values are determined by local government agencies based on a variety of factors, including the property's location, size, age, condition, and recent sales of comparable properties in the area. While tax assessments can be a helpful estimate of a property's value, they are not always accurate and may not reflect the actual market value of your property.

If you have concerns about the accuracy of your property's tax assessment, you may wish to contact your local tax assessor's office and request a review of the assessment. They may be able to provide more information on how the assessment was made and potentially adjust the assessment if necessary.

WHAT HAPPENS IF THE APPRAISED VALUE COMES BACK LOWER THAN THE CONTRACT PRICE?

If the appraised value comes back lower than the contract price in a real estate transaction, it can have a significant impact on the deal.

Firstly, the buyer may be unable or unwilling to pay the difference between the appraised value and the contract price. This can result in the deal falling through unless the seller agrees to lower the price to match the appraised value.

Secondly, if the buyer is using a mortgage to finance the purchase, the lender will typically only lend up to a certain percentage of the appraised value, known as the loan-to-value ratio. If the appraised value is lower than the contract price, the lender may refuse to provide a mortgage for the full contract price, and the buyer will need to come up with additional funds to cover the difference or renegotiate the terms of the deal with the seller.

Alternatively, the buyer and seller may decide to contest the appraisal and request a re-evaluation. The process of getting a second appraisal can be time-consuming and expensive, but it may be necessary to keep the deal on track.

In summary, when the appraised value comes back lower than the contract price, it can cause complications and potential roadblocks in a real estate transaction. However, there are options available to address the issue, including renegotiating the contract price, seeking alternative financing, or requesting a new appraisal.

WHAT IS THE DIFFERENCE BETWEEN A LIST PRICE AND SALE PRICE?

The list price of your home is the initial price that you and your real estate agent have agreed to advertise the property for sale. This is the price that is listed on various real estate websites, in marketing materials, and on the for-sale sign in front of your home.

The sales price, on the other hand, is the final price that you and the buyer have agreed upon through negotiations. It is the price at which the home is actually sold and the money is exchanged between the buyer and seller.

The sales price is typically lower than the list price because buyers will often make an initial offer below the asking price and negotiate with the seller until both parties agree on a mutually acceptable price. The difference between the list price and sales price can vary depending on the local real estate market, the condition of the property, and other factors. In some cases, the sales price may even be higher than the list price if there are multiple competing offers on the property.

SHOULD I PRICE MY HOME ON THE HIGH END, SO I HAVE ROOM TO NEGOTIATE?

It's not always a good strategy to price your home at the high end to leave room for negotiation.

One reason for this is that overpricing your home could potentially turn off potential buyers, who may not even consider it as an option.

This can result in your home sitting on the market for an extended period, which could lead to a lower final selling price than if it had been priced appropriately from the start.

Additionally, overpricing your home could lead to a lack of interest from real estate agents, who may be less motivated to show your home to potential buyers if they believe it's priced too high.

Instead, it's generally recommended to research the local real estate market and work with a professional real estate agent to determine a fair market value for your home. This can help attract potential buyers and lead to a faster and more successful sale, without leaving money on the table.

WHAT IS A LISTING AGREEMENT?

A listing agreement in real estate is a contract between a property owner and a real estate broker or agent that sets out the terms and conditions under which the broker or agent will represent the owner in the sale or lease of a property.

The agreement typically includes details such as the listing price, the length of time the property will be listed, the commission or fee that the broker or agent will receive, and the responsibilities of both parties.

There are different types of listing agreements, including exclusive right to sell, exclusive agency, and open listing agreements. In an exclusive right to sell agreement, the broker or agent has the exclusive right to sell the property during the listing period, regardless of who brings the buyer.

In an exclusive agency agreement, the broker or agent has the exclusive right to sell the property, but the owner retains the right to sell the property without paying a commission if they find a buyer on their own. In an open listing agreement, the owner can list the property with multiple brokers or agents, and only the broker or agent who brings a buyer who closes the sale will receive a commission.

DO I NEED TO HOLD AN OPEN HOUSE TO SELL MY HOME?

No, you do not necessarily need to hold an open house to sell your home. While open houses can be a useful tool for attracting potential buyers and generating interest in your property, they are not a requirement for selling a home.

Some real estate agents and home sellers prefer not to hold open houses due to concerns about security, inconvenience, and the potential for unqualified or disinterested buyers to attend.

Instead of relying solely on open houses, many agents and sellers use a variety of other marketing and advertising techniques to promote their listings, such as online listings, virtual tours, targeted advertising, and networking with other agents and industry professionals.

Ultimately, the decision to hold an open house or not should be based on your specific needs and preferences, as well as the current market conditions in your area. Your real estate agent can provide guidance and advice on the best marketing strategies for your home.

WHAT ARE THE ADVANTAGES OF STAGING A HOME?

Staging a home can have several advantages:

- **Increased visual appeal**: A staged home is designed to look its best and can help potential buyers visualize themselves living in the space. This can make the home more visually appealing and attractive.

- **Better photos and online presence**: When a home is staged, it tends to look better in photos and online listings. This can help attract more potential buyers and generate more interest in the property.

- **Highlighting the home's best features**: Staging can help highlight the best features of a home and draw attention to its unique selling points. This can help potential buyers see the home's value and they'll be more likely to make an offer.

- **Making the space feel larger**: By decluttering and organizing a home, staging can make the space feel larger and more open. This can make it easier for potential buyers to see the full potential of the home.

- **Faster sale**: Staging a home can help it sell faster by making it more appealing to potential buyers. This can be especially important in a competitive real estate market where homes may take longer to sell.

Overall, staging a home can be a smart investment for sellers looking to make their home more appealing to potential buyers and sell it quickly at the best possible price.

What minor improvements can I make that will increase the value of my home?

WHAT HAPPENS IF I GET A LOW OFFER ON MY HOME?

Getting a low offer on your home can be disappointing, but it's important to remember that it's just the starting point of negotiations. Here are some things to consider if you receive a low offer:

- **Don't take it personally**: Remember that the buyer is likely trying to get the best deal possible, and the low offer may not reflect the true value of your home.

- **Evaluate the offer:** Consider the terms of the offer, such as the closing date and contingencies, in addition to the price. If the terms are favorable, it may be worth countering the offer.

- **Respond with a counteroffer**: If you're not happy with the offer, you can respond with a counter-offer that is more in line with your expectations.

This could be a higher price, different closing date, or other terms that are important to you.

- **Keep the lines of communication open**: Be responsive to the buyer's requests for information or negotiations, as this can help keep the process moving forward.

- **Be prepared to walk away**: If you're not able to come to an agreement with the buyer, you may need to consider other options, such as relisting the property or waiting for a better offer.

Remember, the key is to remain objective and flexible throughout the negotiation process, and to work towards a solution that is mutually beneficial for both parties.

WHAT ARE SELLER CONCESSIONS?

Seller concessions refer to the concessions or incentives a seller offers to a buyer during a real estate transaction. These concessions typically involve the seller contributing to the buyer's closing costs or providing other financial incentives to sweeten the deal and make the purchase more appealing to the buyer.

Examples of seller concessions may include covering some or all of the buyer's closing costs, offering a credit towards repairs or upgrades, or reducing the price of the home to make it more affordable for the buyer. The specifics of seller concessions can be negotiated during the real estate transaction and are typically outlined in the purchase contract.

WHAT IS A HOME INSPECTION PHASE?

A home inspection phase typically refers to a process in which a professional inspector examines a property, typically a residential one, to assess its overall condition and identify any potential issues or defects that could affect its value or safety.

During a home inspection, the inspector will typically examine the home's foundation, roof, electrical and plumbing systems, HVAC system, insulation, and other key features.

They will also look for signs of mold, water damage, pest infestations, and other issues that could affect the home's value or pose a health or safety risk to its occupants.

The inspection report generated by the inspector will provide a detailed overview of the findings, including any recommended repairs or improvements that should be made before the property is sold or occupied.

This report can be used by buyers to negotiate repairs or price reductions with the seller or by owners to prioritize repairs and maintenance.

WHAT IS A SALE CONTINGENCY?

A sale contingency in the context of a house sale is a clause that is included in a contract between the buyer and seller, which makes the sale of the house contingent upon the occurrence of a particular event.

Typically, this event is the sale of the buyer's current home. The sale contingency allows the buyer to back out of the contract without any penalty if they are unable to sell their current home within a specified period. It is a common condition that is used to protect buyers from being stuck with two mortgage payments if they are unable to sell their current home before buying a new one.

However, it can also make the sale less attractive to sellers who may prefer to have a more certain sale.

WHAT CLOSING COSTS ARE SELLERS EXPECTED TO PAY?

The closing costs that sellers are expected to pay can vary depending on several factors such as the location, the type of property, and the terms of the sale. However, here are some of the common closing costs that sellers are typically expected to pay:

- **Real estate commission**: This is the fee paid to the real estate agent or broker who facilitated the sale of the property.

- **Transfer taxes and recording fees:** These are fees paid to the local government for transferring ownership of the property and recording the sale.

- **Title insurance**: This is an insurance policy that protects the buyer and lender against any defects or claims on the title of the property.

- **Prorated property taxes:** The seller is responsible for paying property taxes up until the date of closing.

- **Attorney fees:** In some states, it is customary for the seller to pay for an attorney to represent them during the closing process.

- **Home warranty**: The seller may choose to provide a home warranty to the buyer as a way to provide additional protection against unexpected repairs or defects in the home.

- **Prepayment penalties**: If the seller has a mortgage on the property that has a prepayment penalty, they may be responsible for paying that penalty at closing.

It's important to note that the exact closing costs that the seller will be responsible for can vary depending on the specifics of the sale. It's always a good idea for sellers to work closely with their real estate agent or attorney to ensure that they understand all of the costs associated with the sale of their property.

WHAT ARE SOME SIGNS THAT MY HOUSE IS PRICED TOO HIGH?

- **Limited Interest**: If your home has been on the market for an extended period of time with limited interest or showings, it may be a sign that potential buyers consider the price too high.

- **Lack of Offers**: Another sign that your house may be overpriced is the lack of offers. If you have received no offers, or only lowball offers, it may be a sign that your asking price is too high.

- **Low Appraisal Value**: If you receive an appraisal value that is lower than your asking price, it's a clear sign that your home is overpriced.

- **Comparable Listings**: If comparable properties in your area are selling for less, it may be a sign that your home is priced too high.

- **Feedback from Agents and Potential Buyers**: If you consistently receive feedback from agents and potential buyers that the price is too high, it's a sign that you may need to reconsider your asking price.

- **Reductions in Price**: If you have already reduced the price of your home multiple times, it's an indication that your original asking price was too high.

It's important to remember that the real estate market is constantly changing, and pricing a home can be a delicate balancing act. If you are unsure about your home's price, it may be helpful to consult with a local real estate agent to get a professional opinion.

HOW DO I MAKE A FAIR OFFER ON A HOUSE IN A SELLER'S MARKET?

In a seller's market, where demand for homes is high and inventory is low, making a fair offer on a house can be challenging. However, there are a few strategies you can use to make an offer that is fair to both you and the seller:

- **Do your research**: Before making an offer, research the local real estate market to get an idea of the average selling price for homes in the area. This will help you understand the fair market value of the home you're interested in.

- **Work with a real estate agent**: A good real estate agent can provide valuable insight into the local market and help you determine a fair offer price.

- Get pre-approved for a mortgage: A pre-approval letter from a lender can show the seller that you are a serious buyer and have the financial means to purchase the home.

- **Consider making a strong initial offer:** In a seller's market, it may be necessary to make a strong initial offer to stand out from other potential buyers. However, be careful not to offer more than you can afford.

- **Be flexible**: Consider including contingencies in your offer, such as a home inspection or appraisal contingency, to give the seller some peace of mind.

- **Write a personal letter**: In some cases, writing a personal letter to the seller explaining why you love the home and why you would be a good fit for the neighborhood can help you stand out from other potential buyers.

Remember that making a fair offer doesn't necessarily mean offering the full asking price. It means offering a price that reflects the fair market value of the home while taking into account the local real estate market conditions.

MY HOUSE DID NOT SELL USING A REALTOR. WHAT SHOULD I DO?

If your house did not sell with a realtor, there are several things you can do to improve your chances of finding a buyer:

- **Review your pricing strategy**: Consider lowering the price of your house. If it was on the market for a while, it may have been priced too high. You could also consider offering incentives to potential buyers, such as paying for closing costs.

- **Make improvements**: Take a critical look at your house and see if there are any improvements that can be made to make it more attractive to buyers. This could include staging the house, painting, cleaning, or making repairs.

- **Market your property better**: If your realtor didn't do a good job marketing your property, consider hiring a professional photographer to take high-quality photos or creating a virtual tour to showcase your home.

- **Try a different sales method**: You could consider selling your house through a different sales method, such as an auction, a lease-to-own agreement, or selling it yourself (For Sale By Owner).

- **Hire a new realtor**: If you think your realtor didn't do a good job marketing your property, you could consider hiring a new realtor who has a better marketing strategy and more experience selling homes in your area.

Overall, it's important to take a step back and analyze why your house didn't sell. By identifying potential issues and making changes, you can increase your chances of finding a buyer.

HOW DO I SELL MY HOUSE WITHOUT USING A REALTOR?

Selling a house without hiring a realtor can save you money on commissions, but it also requires more work on your part. Here are some steps you can take to sell your house without a realtor:

- **Set the right price**: Research the market to determine the fair market value of your home. You can use online real estate databases to check the prices of similar homes in your area.

- **Prepare your home**: Make necessary repairs, declutter and clean the house, and stage it to make it look its best. Take high-quality photos of the interior and exterior to use in your marketing materials.

- **Market your home**: Use online real estate platforms like Zillow, Redfin, or Realtor.com to list your home for sale. You can also advertise on social media, create flyers, and put up signs in your neighborhood.

- **Show your home**: When potential buyers show interest, schedule showings and be available to answer questions about the property. You can also create a virtual tour of your home to share online.

- **Negotiate and close the sale**: Once you receive an offer, negotiate the price and terms with the buyer. Use a real estate attorney or title company to handle the paperwork and closing process.

Selling a house without a realtor requires more work, but it is possible to do successfully. By following these steps, you can save money and sell your house on your own.

Like I said in the introduction, while this book is packed full of valuable information, it may not have all the answers to all your questions.

So, if you have a question that's not addressed in this book I'm here to help. Feel free to reach out. All my contact information is on the following page.

THE VALUE OF A SELLER'S AGENT

A listing agent, often termed a seller's agent, is a cornerstone in selling a home. Their professional understanding, deep market comprehension, and unwavering dedication safeguard and prioritize the seller's interests. A listing agent enriches the transaction process considerably by offering:

Strategic Pricing: Detailed market analyses determine the most effective listing price, aiming to attract buyers while optimizing your financial gain.

Marketing Mastery: Listing agents deploy customized marketing strategies to increase your home's visibility, targeting potential buyers and maximizing reach.

Home Enhancement Counsel: They advise on or coordinate staging to accentuate your home's appeal, creating a captivating first impression for buyers.

Negotiation Excellence: Seasoned in the art of negotiation, the agent endeavors to procure the best possible terms for you, drawing upon their experience and market acuity.

Professional Liaison: They skillfully manage relationships with photographers, inspectors, contractors, and others to ensure that each aspect of the selling process meets high standards.

Transaction Management: They navigate the transaction's complexities from the initial listing to closing, ensuring a seamless progression.

Legal Compliance: With up-to-date knowledge of legal pertinence, the agent ensures that all sale facets adhere to local laws and regulations.

Dedicated Resources: Full-time agents dedicate their full focus to selling your property, responding proactively to inquisitions and bids. Seven days a week, day and night on Holidays and weekends.

Robust Connections: Their expansive network bolsters the likelihood of a swift sale, with access to a broader pool of buyer's agents and potential purchasers.

Support Beyond the Sale: After the closing, a good listing agent may assist with any subsequent inquiries or requirements.

The distinctive advantage of recruiting a full-time, dedicated listing agent lies in their steadfast commitment to your transaction. Their consistent availability ensures a focused approach to selling your home efficiently and lucratively.

Furthermore, their continuous engagement in the industry endows them with a profound grasp of market dynamics and adeptness in negotiation. With current knowledge of legal standards and efficiency that stems from a full-time focus, such agents leverage their rich networks and resources to the seller's significant benefit. Partnering with a consummate professional aligns with the overarching objective: to sell your property swiftly, adeptly, and at the best possible price.

A listing agent's numerous responsibilities underscore their indispensable role in orchestrating a successful and satisfactory conclusion for home sellers.

When refining the list of things a listing agent does for you, it becomes clear that their involvement is multifaceted and extensive. This illuminates why investing in a seasoned full-time agent is worthwhile, as they transform the intricate real estate transaction into an expedient and rewarding experience for the seller.

ABOUT ANGELA DILORENZO

Angela DiLorenzo is a full-time resident of Traverse City, and she loves living there. She considers Northern Michigan one of the most beautiful places in the United States. It has so much to offer with four seasons and tons of activities. Angela enjoys skiing, boating, riding in the woods on her quad, exercising, reading, and spending quality time with her amazing family.

She obtained her real estate license in 1999 and has a salesperson's license in Florida and a broker's license in Michigan. Angela understands the importance of keeping up with the industry's changes. That is why she continues to educate herself beyond the required training from the state or national level. Over the years, she has earned several professional designations and certifications.

As a Certified Residential Specialist (CRS), Angela is one of only 3% of the active CRS realtors in the country. Along with other national designations and certifications, including GRI (Graduate of the Real Estate Institute), ABR (Accredited Buyer Representative), E-PRO (Advanced Digital Marketing), SRES (Seniors Real Estate Specialist), RSPS (Resort & Second-Home Property Specialist), ALHS (Luxury Home Specialist), CSP (Certified Staging Professional), RENE (Real Estate

Negotiation Expert), CNHE (Certified New Home Specialist) and RCC (Residential Construction Certified).

Her professional memberships include the local Traverse Connect chamber, Aspire North (local Realtor association), NAR (National Association of Realtors), MAR (Michigan Association of Realtors), The Women Leaders Association. Plus, Angela is a Guild member of the Institute for Luxury Home Marketing and an ongoing member of Who's Who in Luxury Real Estate.

Angela believes in excellence, integrity, and transparency; she does not view herself as a salesperson but rather as a resource with the facts, connections, and skill set to help clients make the best decisions for themselves and their families. She can assure clients she will be honest (even if the truth is not what they want to hear) and will work diligently on their behalf because she believes in putting in as much effort needed for the desired results. Therefore, Angela studies the market daily to find any factors or aspects that could be leveraged and prove beneficial in getting the best outcome.

She is proud to be part of Berkshire Hathaway Home Services Michigan. As an associate broker, Angela consistently ranks in the top 1% nationwide. She is the leader of The Michigan Lifestyle Homes Group and the managing broker of the Traverse City office. In addition, Angela is the author of Essential Home Selling

Strategies, what every homeowner needs to know, and the publisher of "The Faces of Grand Traverse County."

The most important part of her business is her clients. Angela loves what she does and how she can help. Her most rewarding moments are when she has achieved her clients' real estate goals. And most of her clients become friends, which is a bonus for her!

WHAT ANGELA'S CLIENTS ARE SAYING

"We are so grateful to have had the chance to work with Angela DiLorenzo in the selling of our home. Her promptness, knowledge of the market, patience and kindness helped ease the process. The amount of time and effort she put in was invaluable and very appreciated! She went the extra mile and was always positive in every step of the way. She was available, dedicated, committed and patient. We felt well taken care of!!"

-Cathy Z.

"Absolutely the greatest in every respect! Our sales experience and Angela in particular did a marvelous job for us."

-Dave and Jan

"My mother was very fortunate to have been referred to Angela DiLorenzo. To her, the thought of selling her house of 29 years as a recent widow was scary and overwhelming but Angela put her at ease immediately. It was obvious that Angela had my mother's best interests in mind throughout the entire process. Angela not only provided guidance on what little work needed to be done on the house, but she also had the resources to accomplish these tasks. And by allowing my mother to dictate the timing of the listing and sale, she helped alleviate much of the stress of this enormous undertaking.

As an experienced real estate agent, Angela provided all of the services that would be considered a given including state-of-the-art marketing, professional photography, market analysis to establish the best list price, etc. But what set Angela apart, was that she went above and beyond. She took a personal interest in my mom during this emotionally charged time. Angela was readily available every step of the way for any questions or concerns. We are both grateful for her professional yet personal, hands-on approach and we highly recommend her to anyone looking to sell their house."

-Kim M.

"We first chose Berkshire Hathaway Real Estate because it is the most prestigious. We then asked for their best realtor who turned out to be Angela DiLorenzo. We immediately knew she was the right one. Angela came to our home on the lake. We knew immediately that we had made the right decision in choosing her. We agreed to the asking price, but after negotiating with two buyers, it went $225,000 over the asking price. Her photographer's video helped bring buyers to our lake property. Angela has a great personality and is extremely knowledgeable. We highly recommend her."

-Roy and Carole

"Angela is without a doubt a consummate professional who handles the details of the search and purchase in a technical yet personal manner. She is excellent in her communication skills and provides her clients with timely and helpful feedback. I can't imagine what this purchase would have been it not for having Angela at our side. I would recommend Angela to anyone interested in any type of real estate transaction. Also, we have come to regard Angela as a trusted friend and hope that will continue long after the purchase."

- Kenneth F

"Angela is just fabulous! She is dedicated to finding the perfect house for her client, answers all questions in a timely manner and just always goes that extra mile."

— Anita F

"Angie is a pleasure to work with! She is a great communicator and always kept us in the loop throughout the whole process! "

— Steve M

"Angela is amazing!! She is personable and so much fun to be around. Moving here from out of state and not knowing the area didn't matter as she made our home-buying experience easy and stress-free. She took the time out of her schedule for one week while we were here to drive us to several homes in the area. We found our forever home!! I cannot thank her enough for her professionalism and knowledge of the Northern Michigan real estate market. I highly recommend her for your Northern Michigan real estate needs!"

— Michael C

"Angela did an excellent job of selling our home very quickly. Angela is very knowledgeable, personable, and professional. I highly recommend her!"

- Tamara P

"Angela is very professional and extremely knowledgeable in ALL aspects of buying and selling Real Estate ...I mean, have you seen her credentials?? The most decorated Realtor I know and she is committed to continuing to be the expert in our field. Her knowledge and experience in Real Estate are one of a kind ~ pair that with her caring approach and you'll see how smooth a real estate transaction can be!"

- Brenda B

"Angela was great! She was very easy to work with and was always available to answer any questions. "

- Rob

"We are so appreciative of the effort and manner in which Angela Dilorenzo helped us sell our home. We highly recommend her for her expertise and professionalism . All her communications were timely and articulate. We were impressed with how fast, as well as how fast efficiently she corresponded with us.

Within days of entering the market she brought us an offer with specifics we requested such as a generous possession date and even a sales price beyond our expectations! Her kind, friendly manner made the selling transaction good smoothly. We certainly recommend her to any prospective seller or buyer."

- Lenore G

"Angela Dilorenzo did a five-star job. We are so appreciative of the effort and manner in which she helped us sell our house. We highly recommend her for her expertise and professionalism. All her communications were timely and informative.

We were impressed with how fast as well as how efficiently she corresponded with us. Within days of entering the market, she brought us an offer with specifics we requested such as a generous possession date and a sales price beyond our expectations! Her kind, friendly manner made the selling transaction go smoothly. We certainly recommend her to any prospective seller or buyer."

- Jim G

"Great job. Angela is very personable and a pleasure to work with"

- Kathy W

"Angela was a wonderful realtor. She was prompt and always answered our questions in a timely manner. She made the buying experience easy and accommodated our needs when things were confusing. Thank you very much for your time. "

- Paul L

"Coming from New England we were so lucky to have Angela as our buyers' agent. She is outstanding! She's deeply knowledgeable, personable, resourceful, an excellent communicator and very kind. Maybe that last trait, always underrated, is most important. We highly recommend her — especially in tough markets. She is detail-oriented but also has great intuition about people and their needs and likes. Finding the right house is a science and an art and she understands that. "

\- Andrea S

"Angela did a great job for me. We had some problems with my lender and she went above and beyond to solve the problems. We were able to solve the problems with her help. Thanks, Angela. "

\- Abel E

"Angela is hands down the most professional, hardworking, knowledgeable Realtor I have ever met. You will know she genuinely cares about helping you make the right decision for you and your family the minute you meet her."

\- Patti C

"Par Excellance'. Totally professional, immense drive, very polite (and well groomed)."

- Carole C

"Angela was outstanding in the sale of my property. Excellent usage of aerial photography to create a great property portfolio."

-David W.

"Angela is great! Thorough and persistent all through the sales process. "

- Dennis W

www.ingramcontent.com/pod-product-compliance
Lightning Source LLC
Chambersburg PA
CBHW071858200326
41519CB00016B/4450